An Unauthorized Guide to

Rugrats® Collectibles

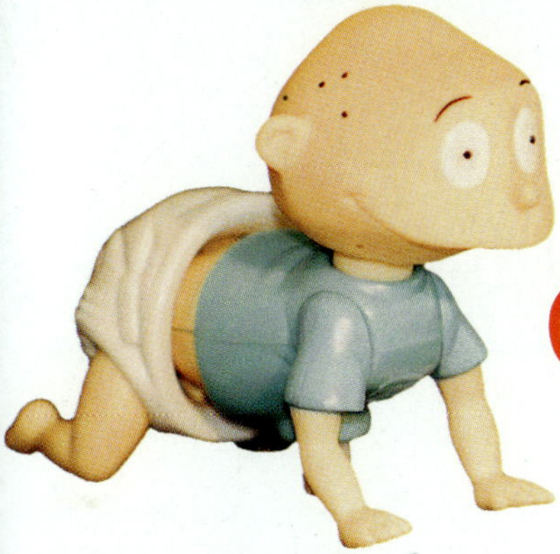

Jan Lindenberger

I0809081

Schiffer® Publishing Ltd

4880 Lower Valley Road, Atglen, PA 19310 USA

"Muddy Angelica" 100% nylon bath rug. 19" x 29".
Viacaom International Inc. Made in Egypt. $15-20

Title page:
Bottom left: Stuffed velour Angelica doll. 27". Mattel. $30-40
Top left: Tommy, plastic wind-up crawler. $4-5
Center right: Cotton stuffed pillow, Chuckie. 13". $10-15

Library of Congress Catalog Card Number: 99-61131

Designed by Bonnie M. Hensley
Type set in Kids/Korinna BT

ISBN: 0-7643-0877-7
Printed in China
1 2 3 4

Published by Whitford Press
A Division of Schiffer Publishing, Ltd.
4880 Lower Valley Road
Atglen, PA 19310 USA
Phone: (610) 593-1777 Fax: (610) 593-2002
E-mail: schifferbk@aol.com
Please visit our web site catalog at
www.schifferbooks.com
or write for a free catalog.
This book may be purchased from the publisher.
Please include $3.95 postage.
Try your bookstore first.

In Europe, Schiffer books are distributed by
Bushwood Books
6 Marksbury Avenue
Kew Gardens
Surrey TW9 4JF England
Phone: 44 (0)181 392-8585;
Fax: 44 (0)181 392-9876
E-mail: Bushwd@aol.com

We are interested in hearing from authors with book ideas on related subjects.

Contents

Acknowledgments 4
Introduction 5
Bibliography 6
Dolls 7
Figures and Playsets 25
Games, Puzzles and Toys 35
Kitchen, Bed and Bath 48
Watches, Jewelry and Keychains 62
Wardrobe 74
Bags and Totes 95
Books and Videos 103
Partytime and Holidays 112
Schooltime 126
Premiums and Advertising 143
Other Rugrat Collectibles not Shown 159

The Rugrats Gang is waiting for you!
Tommy Pickles has a mission.
Chuckie is worrying about it.
Phil and Lil are ready to go.
Angelica has a master plan to sabotage it.
Tommy's loyal mutt, Spike, is ready to save the day.
As soon as the grown-ups turn their backs...
Let your Rugrat adventures begin.

—From the Back of the Rugrats Doll Package

Fleece jogging sweatsuit. Embroidered Rugrats on front. $20-25 set.

Acknowledgments

A special thanks to my grand daughter Ashley Lindenberger for helping search out the information for this first Rugrats collectible book. As a twelve-year-old she watched *Rugrats* on TV and the *Rugrats Movie,* which gave her much of the information.

Ashley Lindenberger (Granddaughter of the author) holding satin Chuckie Finster stuffed pillow doll. $25-30

Introduction

Welcome to the world of the Rugrats, where everything is big and where the Rugrat gang enters into new adventures every day! Where they stick together and aren't afraid to venture out and explore the unusual and challenging things that tempt their curiosity. Collecting the Rugrats tugs on your heart strings as they are a fun, positive bunch of kids who live in a fun, positive world. The adults and kids alike deal with regular situations and crises of everyday families. There is no situation too violent for the babies or too juvenile for the adults. And they all handle it with a positive attitude and good always comes in the end.

Since these collectibles came on the market in early 1991 (when the TV program was produced, building to a full-length movie in 1998) they have been become a fun, much-desired collectible. Newer items such as the PVC figures of Tommy wearing his diaper, Angelica with her doll, Chuckie wearing his glasses, and Reptar the dinosaur sold in department stores everywhere, along with dolls, games, jewelry, toys, clothes, videos, and much more! Burger King fast food restaurants even had a promotion where they gave free toys with their kids' meals (Feruary 23rd thru March 29, 1998). They included "Hero of the Universe" Tommy, a plastic wind-up toy. The "Jumping Chuckie" toy jumps around on his toy bunny. There's also "Tandem Triking Phil & Lil" (Phil & Lil on their big wheel), "Wind Blown Angelica" (Angelica in her toy convertible), and "Reptar Alive" (a walking Reptar). There was also a 4-page magazine with cut-out signs—hope you kept that too! When collectibles are in limited quanities or only given or sold for a short time, like the Burger King items, one should assume they will become very collectible.

I collect the Rugrats not just because of their potential collector value, but for the colorful cute kids they really are! After all, with a show that has won outstanding awards since 1991, why not?

I hope you enjoy this Rugrats information and price guide. It is meant to be used as a guide only and will show you the prices commanded on today's collectibles market. Please use it on your Rugrat hunt and remember prices may vary from state to state and whether it purchased from flea markets, garage sales, shops, or auctions. Also condition is a great factor. I hope you have fun in your "search" and have as much fun using this guide as much as I did putting it together. I have been asked "why the Rugrats?" I can only respond as Tommy would say, "A baby's gotta do what a baby's gotta do."

Thanks, Jan Lindenberger

Bibliography

Graham, Jefferson. *The Ultimate Rugrats Fan Book*. New York: Simon & Schuster, 1998.

This wonderful, well-written book taught me a lot about the Rugrats and is required reading for any Rugrats fan! Graham has been on the staff of *USA Today* since 1984 and is also a photographer residing in Los Angeles, California.

Dolls

Chuckie Finster doll with rubber head, arms, legs, and stuffed body. Wet the popsicle and Chuckie's face gets dirty. Washable face. Mattel. 11". $20-30

Angelica Pickles doll with rubber head, arms, legs, and stuffed body. Wet the popsicle and Angelica's face gets dirty. Washable face. Mattel. 11". $20-30

Tommy Pickles doll with rubber head, arms, legs, and stuffed body. Wet the popsicle and Tommy's face gets dirty. Washable face. Mattel. 11". $20-30

Chuckie Finster doll with rubber head, arms, legs, and stuffed body. Wet the popsicle and his face gets dirty. Washable face. 2nd edition. Mattel. 11". $20-30

Tommy and Angelica Pickles dolls with rubber head, arms, legs, and stuffed body. Wet the popsicle and their faces get dirty. Washable faces. Mattel. 11". $20-30 each.

Angelica doll with rubber head, arms, legs, and stuffed body. Mattel. 11". $20-30

Plush stuffed Spike doll. Mattel. 11". $20-30

Tommy doll with rubber head, arms, legs, and stuffed body. Mattel. 11". $20-30

Bathtime Tommy with rubber head and stuffed body. Washable. Mattel. 11". $15-20

Bathtime Angelica with rubber head and stuffed body. Mattel. Washable. 11". $15-20

Slumber Party Tommy Pickles doll with rubber head and stuffed body. Mattel. 11". $15-20

Slumber Party Angelica Pickles with rubber head and stuffed body. Mattel. 11". $15-20

Plush Slumber Party Reptar doll. Mattel. 11". $15-20

Plush Slumber Party Chuckie Finster doll. Mattel. 13". $15-20

Rubber Hair-Raising Angelica Pickles doll. Squeeze her tummy and her pigtails spin and she whistles. Mattel. 14". $25-35

Rubber Giggling Tommy Pickles doll. Squeeze his tummy and he giggles and raises his arms. Mattel. 11". $25-35

Rubber Scared Chuckie Finster doll. Pull the spider and he screams and shakes. Mattel. 13". $25-35

Rubber Angelica doll. Squeeze her sides for skating arm action. Mattel. 14". $25-35

Crying Baby Dil Pickles doll, squeeze his tummy and he cries. Mattel. 13". $25-35

Rubber head, hands, feet, stuffed body. To the Rescue Tommy Pickles doll. Squeeze his tummy and he cracks his jump rope whip. Mattel. 13". $25-35

Phil and Lil Deville dolls with rubber head and velour body. 11". Mattel. $25-35 pair

Baby Dil Pickles doll with rubber head and velour body. Put the pacifier in his mouth to stop his hiccups and take it out for baby talk. Battery operated. Mattel. 14". $40-45

Super Singing Tommy Pickles with rubber head and soft body. Press his tummy and he tells stories. Squeeze his hand and he sings. 15". Battery operated. Mattel. $40-45

Stuffed velour Tommy doll. 24". Mattel. $30-40

Stuffed velour Baby Dil doll. 26". Mattel. $30-40

Stuffed velour Chuckie doll. 24". Mattel. $30-40

Stuffed velour Angelica doll. 27". Mattel. $30-40

Cotton Angelica, Chuckie, Tommy bean bag friends. Approx. 8". $6-10 each.

Chuckie bean bag friend, velour. 8". $6-10

Tommy bean bag friend, velour. 8". $6-10

Original display box for bean bag friends. Great graphics. $20-35

Chuckie, Angelica, Tommy. Polyester fiber bean bag heads. 4" x 5". Play By Play. $5-7 each.

Polyester fiber-filled Tommy pillow doll. 19". $25-30

Polyester fiber-filled Angelica pillow doll. 24". $25-30

Polyester fiber filled Chuckie pillow doll. 4". $25-30

Polyester fiber filled Spike pillow doll. $25-30

Velour Angelica hand puppet. Arco Toys. Mattel. $20-25

Velour Tommy hand puppet. Arco Toys. Mattel. $20-25

Velour Chuckie hand puppet. Arco Toys. Mattel. $20-25

Velour Reptar hand puppet. Arco Toys. Mattel. $20-25

Velour Spike toy. Mattel. $15-20

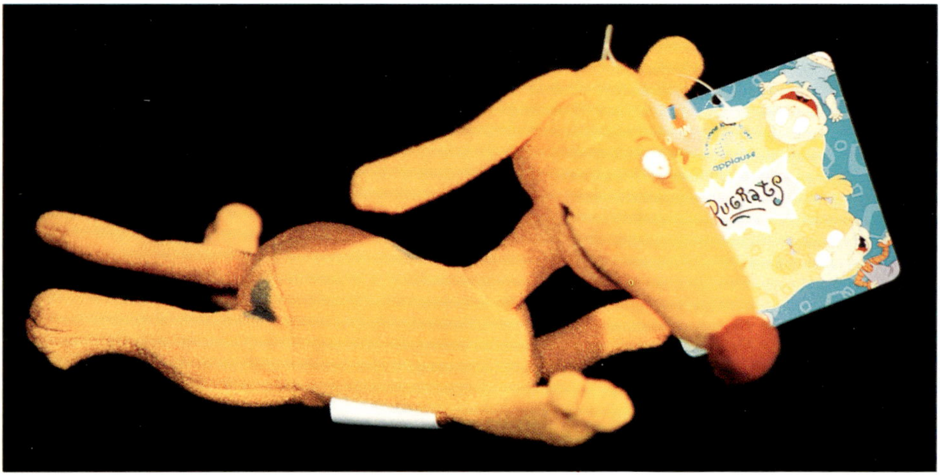

Plush Reptar with plastic eyes. 22". $30-35

Plush velour Reptar. About 8". $10-15

Figures and Playsets

Lil, Tommy, and Chuckie collectible figures. Rubber head, arms, legs, and stuffed body. 4.5". Mattel. $7-10 each.

Angelica. Rubber head, arms, legs, and stuffed body. 4". Mattel. $7-10

Spike, rubber. 4". Mattel. $7-10

Back of box, from previous page, shows figures available.

Baby Dil and Tommy figures. Rubber head, hands, feet, and soft body. 5". Mattel. $7-10 each.

Chuckie and Lil figures. Rubber head, hands, feet, and soft body. 5". Mattel. $7-10 each.

Angelica and Phil figures. Rubber head, hands, feet, and soft body. 5". Mattel. $7-10 each.

Plastic figures. Chuckie and Tommy. 3". Mattel. $4-6 each.

Plastic figures. Lil and Phil. 3". Mattel. $4-6 each.

Plastic figure. Baby Dil with Reptar. Mattel. $4-6

Rubber Dil with bear and Chuckie with monkey playsets. 3". Mattel. $6-8 each.

Rubber Angelica with binoculars play set. 4". Mattel. $6-8

Rugrats figurine set. Spike, Angelica, Tommy, Chuckie. $10-15 set.

Tommy, plastic wind-up crawler. $4-5

Rubber Pickles family set. Mattel. $15-20 set.

Angelica's family set. Rubber head and soft body. Mattel. $15-20 set.

Rubber Pickles grandparents set. Mattel. $15-20 set.

Rugrats Toon Team. Plush Tommy, Angelica, Reptar. Stuffed soft huggable dolls. Velcro palms. 6" to 8". Mattel. $15-20 set.

Rugrats Toon Team. Plush Chuckie, Dil, baby monkey. Stuffed soft huggable dolls with velcro palms and plastic eyes. 6". Mattel. $15-20

Rugrats Toon Team. Plush Tommy, Phil, Top Hat. Soft bodies, velcro palms with plastic eyes. 6". Mattel. $15-20

Rugrats Toon Team. Plush Angelica, Lil, Susie. Soft body with plastic eyes. 6". Mattel. $15-20

Plush Phil with monkey in Monkey Express plastic train. Front and back of box. Mattel. $15-20

Plush Lil with monkey in plastic circus car. Front and back of box. Mattel. $15-20

Plastic Baby Dil's World play set. Rubber Baby Dil and accessories. Mattel. $10-15

Plastic Tommy's World play set. Rubber Tommy and accessories. Mattel. $10-15

Games, Puzzles and Toys

Bump and Bust Out 3-D Game. Mattel. $7-10

Back Yard Toy Hunt Game. Mattel. $7-10

Lookie! Cookies! Game. Mattel. $7-10

My Size 46-piece puzzle, Tommy. 23.5" x 36.5". Liquid to glue puzzle included. Mattel. $8-10

My Size 46-piece puzzle, Chuckie. 23.5" x 36.5". Liquid to glue puzzle included. Mattel. $8-10

8-piece Woodboard puzzle, Angelica. Mattel. $5-8

8-piece Woodboard Reptar puzzle. Mattel. Back shows others available. $5-8

Plastic Tommy's Liquid Magic Window Art activity set. In and out of the package. 12" x 14". $15-20

Plastic activity case with poster and puzzle projects. 11" x 14". $15-20

Plastic stamp and sticker activity set. 9" x 11". $15-20

Plastic sticker treasure kit with carrying case. $8-12

Plastic electronic coin bank. Tommy and Chuckie sitting on Spike. Spike rocks back and forth. MGA Entertainment. 8" x 10". $20-30

Plastic Reptar wagon stamper activity case. 14" x 11". $20-25

Plastic radio controlled walkie talkie Reptar wagon with "Sponsitility" transmitter. $35-40

Plastic Reptar wagon gift set. 10" x 5". $10-15

Plastic Reptar wagon, remote controlled. Mattel. 4" x 6". Battery operated. $15-20

Plastic talking Reptar wagon. Mattel. $20-30

Rubber Tommy bank. $20-25

Plastic walkie talkies. Chuckie is 9". Tommy is 7". MGA Entertainment. $30-40

Rubber Tommy squeezable flashlight. 5". MGA Entertainment. $8-12

Rubber Chuckie squeezable flashlight. 5". $10–15.

Plastic flicker flasher game. Electronic memory reaction game. $15-20

Plastic electronic LCD game. Tiger Premier games. Made in China. $20-30

Giga "Pets Plus" LCD game. Also came as Giga Farm game, Giga Pound game, Giga Circus game. Tiger electronics. $15-20 each.

Plastic toy tag electronic game. Tiger electronics. Made in China. $20-25

Electronic talking Tommy room guard. Says over 30 phrases. Think Way Toys. $30-40

Opposite page:
Top: Plastic ride-on Reptar wagon. Rand. $30-40

Center: Deluxe vinyl playhouse. In the shape of the Reptar wagon. 52" x 32" x 27.5". $40-50

Bottom: Vinyl playhouse. Decorated with the Rugrats. 52"x 32". $25-30

View master reel. (3 reels). Fisher Price. $3-4

R-116
THE
Rugrats
MOVIE
Reptar
Ride On
· Rugrats Reptar Wagon Replica
· Indestructible Plastic Body
· Rugged 6" X 3" Wheels
· Plug-in Reptar Handlebar
Arms & Eyes
· Featuring Tommy, Chuckie & Dil
Ages 18 months - 4 years
Made in U.S.A.
RAND

THE
Rugrats
MOVIE
Deluxe
Play House
Great For Hours Of Fun!

NICKELODEON
Rugrats
Play House
Interior Elastic Cord Keeps All
Poles Connected For Easy Assembly!

Kitchen, Bed and Bath

Plastic talking cups. Press the button and Chuckie says "Go little kid go", Tommy says "I gotta idea", Angelica says "That's Boss Angelica, to you". Each comes with a twist-off lid, straw, and three button cell batteries. $10-15 each.

Plastic and rubber laserware mug. Raised Rugrats design. $7-10 each.

Plastic face mugs. Tommy, Chuckie, Angelica. $6-8 each.

PLACE
STAMP
HERE

SCHIFFER PUBLISHING LTD
4880 LOWER VALLEY ROAD
ATGLEN, PA 19310-9717

Plastic dinnerware set. Plate, bowl, tumbler. Great graphics. Viacom. $15-20 set.

Plastic sports tumbler with lid and straw. $6-8

Fork and spoon set. Plastic-handled metal fork and spoon.$5-7 set.

Plastic straws with rubber figures. Chuckie, Baby Dil, Tommy. $5-7 each.

Plastic sandwich bags. Two different designs. $3-4 each.

Cotton stuffed pillow, Tommy. 13". $10-15

Cotton stuffed pillow, Tommy with ball. 13". $10-15

Cotton stuffed pillow, Chuckie. 13". $10-15

Cotton stuffed pillow, Angelica and Tommy. 13". $10-15

Cotton stuffed pillow, Tommy lying on ball. 13". $10-15

Kid Care bandages, 25 strips with Rugrats graphics. $2-3

Oral-B toothpaste. Blue fruit flavor. $3-4

Kid Care fruit flavor lip balm. 1.5 oz. $3-4

Kids Choice glycerin soap. Tommy and Phil embedded in soap. $5-7 each.

Kid Care punch flavor lip balm. Rubber Tommy sits on top of stick. $3-4

Kid Care mild formula bubble bath. 16 oz. $3-4

Kid Care bubble bath with plastic Tommy sitting on top of bottle. $7-10

Plastic Reptar wagon brush and toothpaste holder. Includes toothbrush and toothpaste. Oral-B. $8-10

Bath bubbles with rubber Angelica hand puppet. $7-10

Bath bubbles with rubber Tommy hand puppet. $7-10

Kid Care body painting soap set. Includes blue and green paint with two sponges and tray. $7-10

Plastic toothbrush. Chuckie holding balloons with Tommy. $3-4

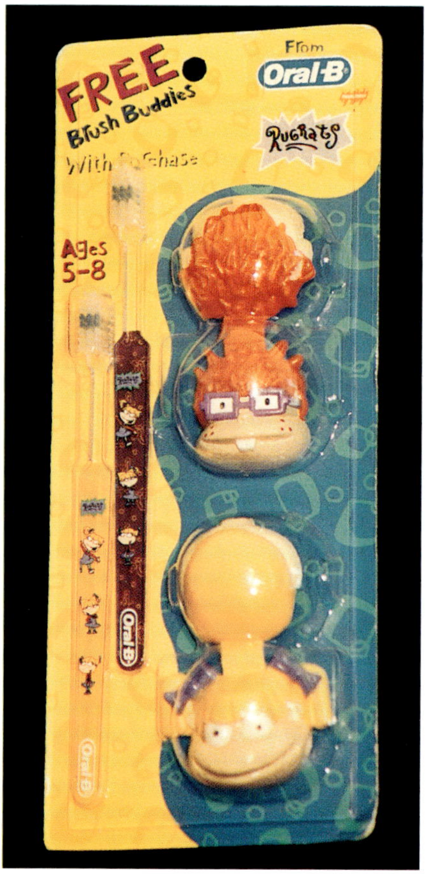

Plastic "Brush Buddies" with purchase of toothbrush. Plastic heads of Tommy and Angelica fit on toothbrush. Oral-B. $4-6

Plastic toothbrush. Graphics of the Rugrats on handle.Oral-B. $3-4

Plastic toothbrush, Tommy hugging Spike. $4-6

Vinyl shower curtain with Chuckie, Tommy, Angelica graphics. 70" x 72". $15-20

Plastic travel tote. Toothbrush, hairbrush, comb, cup, one package of tissues, soap case, mini soap in plastic case. $7-10

Standard size cotton pillow case. Springs Home. $4-6

Two-piece terrycloth towel and washcloth set. $6-10 set

Cotton twin sheet set. Springs Home. $15-20

Polyester comforter. Springs Home. $30-40

Child's polyester indoor sleeping bag. Tommy, Chuckie, Angelica graphics. Springs Home. $25-30

Child's polyester indoor sleeping bag. Springs Home. The Rugrats riding in Reptar wagon print. $25-30

Top: "Real pals" 100% nylon bath rug. 19" x 29". Viacom International Inc. Made in Egypt. $15-20
Center: "Pretty Angelica" 100% nylon bath rug. 19" x 29". Viacom International Inc. Made in Egypt. $15-20
Bottom: "Running from Reptar" 100% nylon bath rug. 19" x 29". Viacom International Inc. Made in Egypt. $15-2

Top: "Muddy Angelica" 100% nylon bath rug. 19" x 29". Viacaom International Inc. Made in Egypt. $15-20

Center: "Be Brave" 100% nylon bath rug. 19" x 29". Viacom International Inc. Made in Egypt. $15-20

Angelica, Chuckie, Tommy 100% nylon bath rug. Viacom International Inc. Made in Egypt. $15-20

Watches, Jewelry and Keychains

Rugrats holiday watch. Tommy in green outfit on face. $15-20

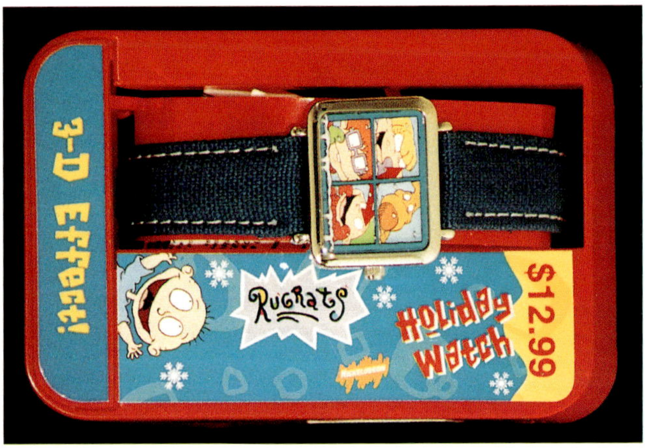

Rugrats holiday watch. 3-D effect. Angelica, Spike, Chuckie, Tommy on face. $15-20

Rugrats holiday watch with glitter strap. Tommy and Chuckie on face. $15-20

Rugrats holiday watch. Metallic dial. Angelica on face. $15-20

Plastic light and sound watch. Tommy and Chuckie spin around the control panel with sounds and flashing lights. $15-20

Plastic mix and match 3-D watch with interchangeable character bands. $15-20

Rugrat watch with iredescent face. Great graphics on band. $15-20

Metal pin-back buttons. Win Craft. $6-10 set.

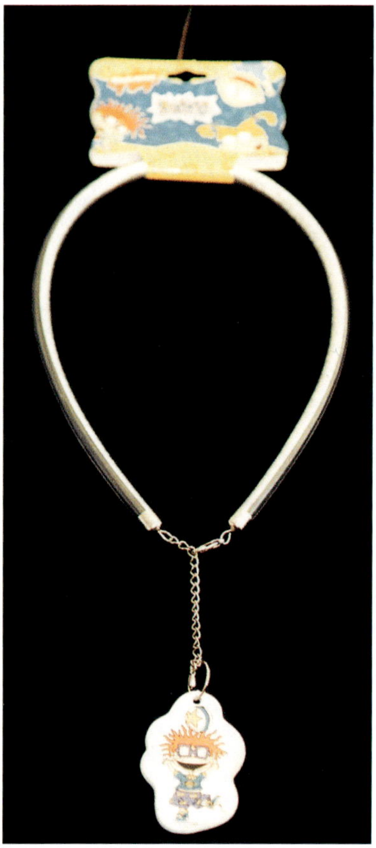

Plastic necklace with dangling Chuckie. Fantasia Accessories Ltd., N.Y. $5-6

Plastic necklace with star that opens and mirror inside. Metal chain. Fantasia Accessories Ltd., N.Y. $5-6

Plastic star ring with chain necklace. Fantasia Accessories Ltd., N.Y. $5-7

Plastic notebook necklace. Fantasia Accessories Ltd., N.Y. $5-7

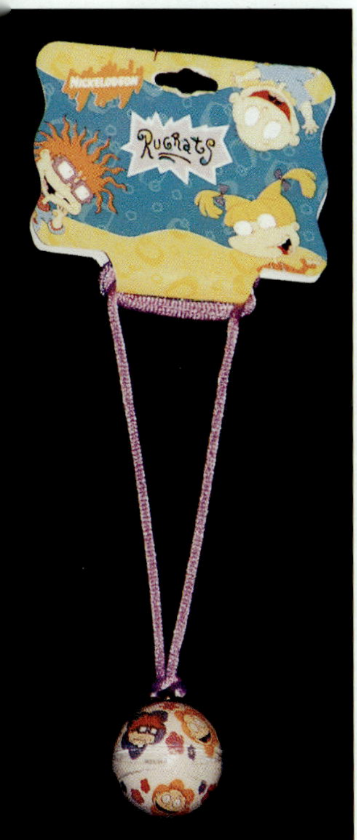

Plastic water-filled rotating ball necklace. Fantasia Accessories Ltd., N.Y. $4-5

Plastic star ring that opens to show mirror. Fantasia Accessories Ltd., N.Y. $4-5

Plastic rings. Chuckie, Phil and Lil, Angelica, Tommy. Fantasia Accessories Ltd., N.Y. $5-7

Plastic water-filled rotating ball ring. Fantasia Accessories Ltd., N.Y. $4-5

Plastic "seven days a week" rings and earrings. Fantasia Accessories Ltd., N.Y. $4-5

Plastic water-filled rotating ball ring. Fantasia Accessories Ltd., N.Y. $4-5

Plastic bracelet with dangling Tommy and Chuckie charms. $4-5 each.

Sterling silver jewelry set with rubber Phil keyring. $10-15

Sterling silver jewelry set with rubber Dil keyring. $10-15

Sterling silver jewelry set with rubber Angelica keyring. $10-15

Sterling silver jewelry set with rubber Tommy keyring. $10-15

Cardboard musical jewelry box. Open and Angelica dances and plays music. $10-15

Cardboard musical jewelry box. Open and Angelica dances and plays music. $10-15

Box that music box came in. Great graphics.

Wooden musical jewelry box. Viacom. $8-10

Cardboard jewelry box with top view. 4" x 6". $7-9

Rubber Reptar friction toy and key ring. 3". Basic Fun. $5-7

Rubber Tommy with removable bottle that really squirts, toy and key ring. Basic Fun. $5-7

Toy and key ring. Rubber Chuckie has removable glasses that change expressions when tilted. Basic Fun. $5-7

Toy and keyring. Rubber Angelica with removable Cynthia doll. Basic Fun. $5-7

Toy and key ring. Rubber poseable Spike. Basic Fun. $5-7

Toy and key ring. Rubber Phil and Lil with "attract and repel" magnetic action, Basic Fun. $5-7

Back of toy and key ring package.

Rubber change purses that open in the back when squeezed. Also key rings. Tommy, Chuckie, Angelica. $7-10 each.

Rubber Spike the dog key ring. $6-8

Wardrobe

Angelica "Shirley Lock Holmes" 100% acrylic knit sweater. $20-30

Angelica print girl's turtleneck shirt. $10-15

Angelica and monkeys print cotton sweatshirt. "You got anything good to eat in this dump!" $10-15

"We're off to see the lizard" cotton sweatshirt. $10-15

"We're Doomed" cotton sweatshirt. Rugrats riding in Reptar wagon. $10-15

Girl's fleece sweatshirt. Embroidered Rugrats and "We're the good guys" printed on front. $15-20

Girl's fleece sweatshirt. Embroidered Rugrats and "So you've decided to learn from the master" printed on front. $15-20

Girl's cotton overalls with Chuckie, Angelica, and Tommy embroidered on front. $15-20

Cotton overalls and shirt, embroidered Tommy on front. $15-20

Cotton overalls and shirt. Embroidered Angelica on bib. "Next to me, you're the cutest little girl here". $15-20

Cotton jumper and shirt. Angelica yelling "I'm not a baby!!!". $15-20

Cotton jumper and shirt. "Mine, mine, everything is mine". $15-20

Cotton jumper and shirt. Embroidered Chuckie, Tommy, Angelica on front. $15-20

Corduroy bib overalls. Embroidered Angelica, "No more mister nice guy". $20-25

Cotton girl's sleep set. Printed pattern of Angelica holding her Cynthia doll. $10-15

Cotton girl's sleep set. Printed pattern of the Rugrats. $10-15

Cotton girl's sleep set. Printed pattern of Angelica playing dress-up. "Don't I look pretty?" Tommy on pants. $10-15

Polyester girl's zip-up sleeper. Printed-on Rugrats pattern. $10-15

Fleece jogging sweatsuit. Embroidered Rugrats on front. $20-25 set.

Fleece shirt and pants pajamas with printed-on Angelica and "It's as clear as the nose on my plate". $15-20

Cotton and polyester boy's shirt. Embroidered Chuckie goalie. "Team Rugrats". $10-15

Polyester Team Rugrat #21 shirt and pants. $15-20 set.

Cotton sweatshirt and pants set. Embroidered Tommy and Chuckie. $20-25

Boy's cotton pajamas with printed Tommy playing basketball on front.

Cotton sweatshirt and pants with embroidered Tommy and Chuckie playing basketball with Reptar. $20-25

Cotton fleece boy's pajamas, zip-up front. Printed Tommy playing soccer. $15-20

Cotton boy's underwear and package. Three in pack. $5-7

Boy's cotton shorts with printed Tommy and Chuckie. $8-10

Waffle weave girl's underwear. Printed Angelica designs. $7-8

Knit hat with embroidered Chuckie and Spike. Simon Spotlight. $5-7

Knit hat and gloves. Embroidered Chuckie. Simon Spotlight. $8-10 set

Knit hat and gloves. Embroidered Tommy. Simon Spotlight. $8-10 set

Vinyl raincoat, front and back. Painted-on Rugrats. $15-20

Cotton color it, iron it, wear it, wash it, tee shirt. #904: Group with logo. $8-12

Cotton color it, iron it, wear it, wash it, tee shirt. #906: Fun ball. $8-12

Cotton color it, iron it, wear it, wash it, tee shirt. #902: Cookies. $8-12

Cotton color it, iron it, wear it, wash it, tee shirt. #905: Box of fun. $8-12

Nylon stretch socks. Chuckie and Tommy. $4-5

Nylon stretch socks. Tommy. $4-5

Nylon stretch socks. Made in Korea. $4-5

Plush slippers with rubber Angelica head. $10-15

Plush slippers with rubber Angelica and Tommy heads. These came as a pair. $10-15

Girl's sneakers with embroidered Angelica, and box. Back of box has punch out tokens to trade. $10-15

Boy's sneakers with embroidered Spike, Chuckie, and Tommy with box. $10-15

Boy's sneakers with embroidered Tommy and Chuckie with box. $10-15

Top and bottom of shoe box. Great graphics. $5-7

Child's rubber snow boots, fleece-lined. $20-25

Bags and Totes

Plastic shoulder bag, Angelica. $8-10

Plastic shoulder bag, Tommy. $8-10

Denim embroidered purse. Chuckie, Angelica, Tommy. $7-10

Vinyl lunch tote with the Rugrats painted on front and back. 7" x 10". $10-15

Vinyl tote. Rugrats on front and back. 5.5". $8-10

Vinyl tote with Rugrats in Reptar wagon. Has attached plastic compass key ring. 9". $10-15

Denim lunch tote with embroidered Tommy, Chuckie, Angelica. $10-15

Vinyl travel case with wheels. Rugrats in Reptar wagon design. 12" x 17". $25-30

Vinyl travel case with wheels. 12" x 17". $25-30

Vinyl backpack. Angelica smelling flowers. 11" x 14". $15-20

Vinyl backpack. Tommy and Baby Dil. 11" x 15". $15-20

Vinyl backpack. Angelica, Tommy, Chuckie. Place to insert ID card on front. 11". $10-15

Vinyl backpack. Rugrats in Reptar wagon. 14" x 12". $10-15

Fabric backpack with painted-on Chuckie. 14" x 17". $15-20

Fabric backpack with painted-on Tommy. 14" x 12". $15-20

Fabric backpack with painted-on Angelica. 14" x 12". $15-20

Vinyl backpack with attached change purse. 11". $10-15

Vinyl backpack with Baby Dil. 11". $10-15

Vinyl backpack with attached play compass and keyring. 9". $10-15

Vinyl backpack with attached change purse. Rugrats on front. 11". $10-1 5

Vinyl backpack with transparent front. 4". $15-20

Books and Videos

Where The Sharks Are paper back book by Duncan Maxfield. $4-5

Stormy Weather book by Molly Wigand. $4-5

Junk, Sweet Junk book by Molly Wigand. $4-5

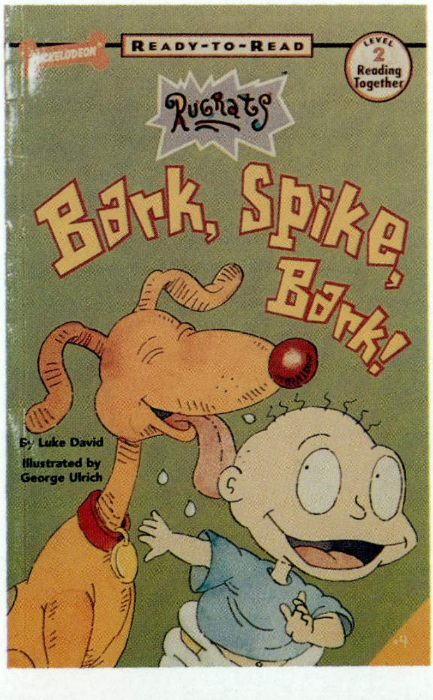

Bark, Spike, Bark! book by Luke David. $4-5

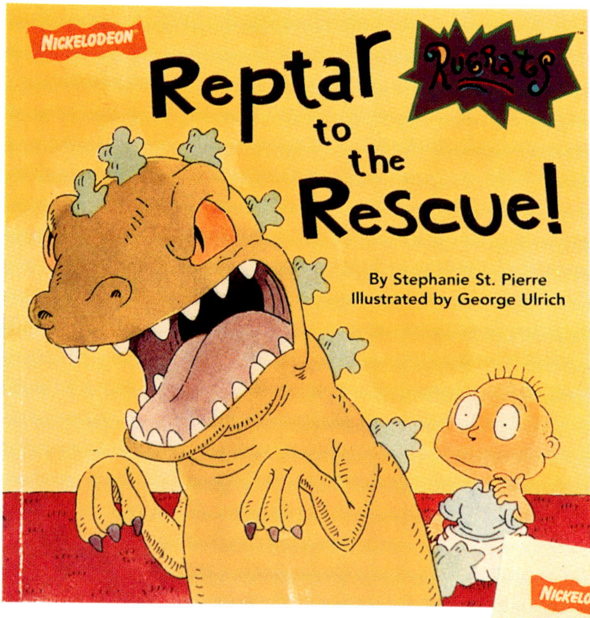

Reptar To The Rescue! book by Stephanie St. Pierre. $4-5

Rugrats Blast Off! book by Stephanie St. Pierre. $4-6

The Bestest Mom book by Susan Hood. $4-6

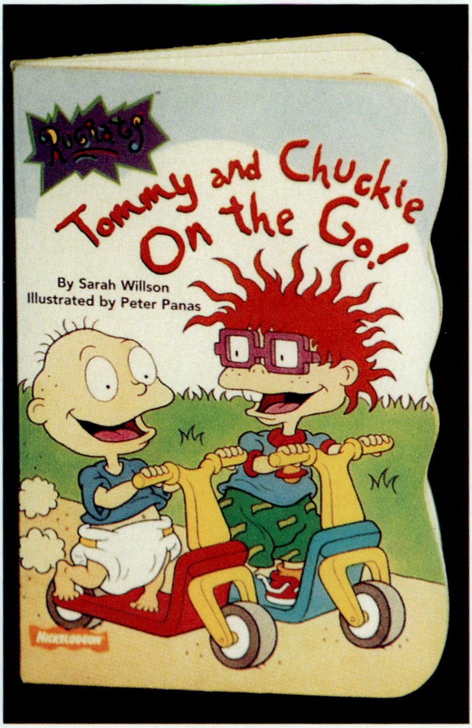

Tommy And Chuckie On The Go! book by Sarah Wilson. $4-6

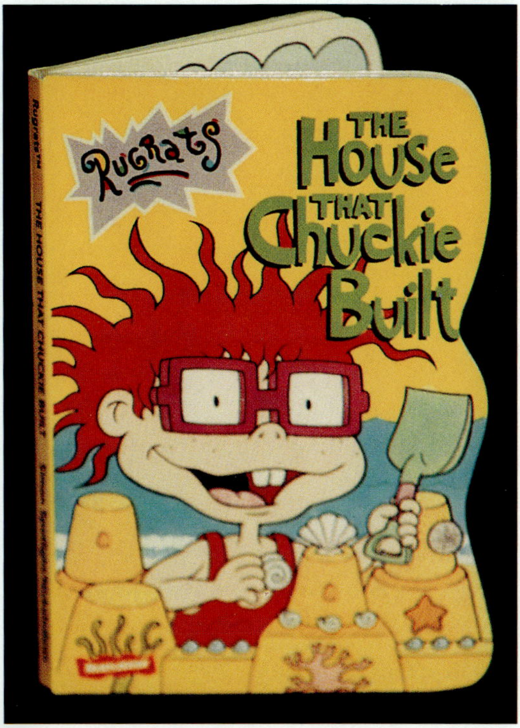

The House That Chuckie Built book by Sarah Wilson. $4-6

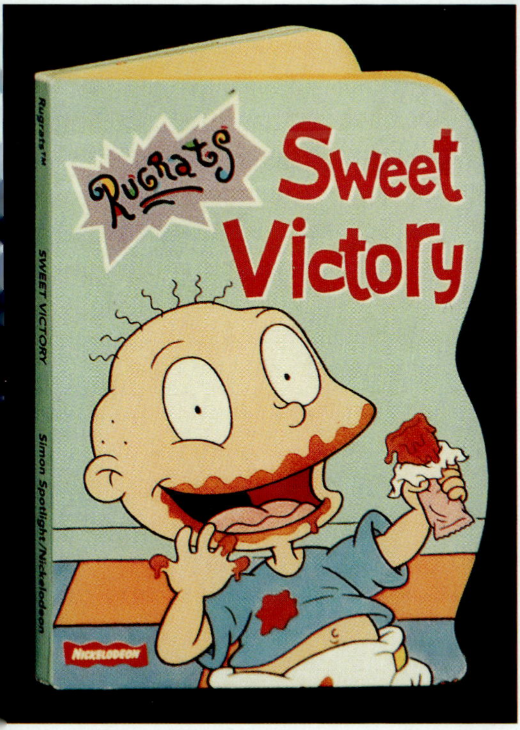

Sweet Victory book by Sarah Wilson. $4-6

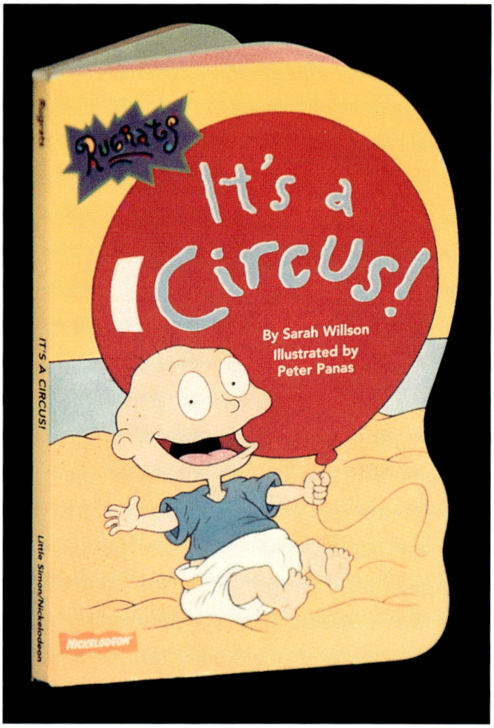

It's A Circus! book by Sarah Wilson. $5-6

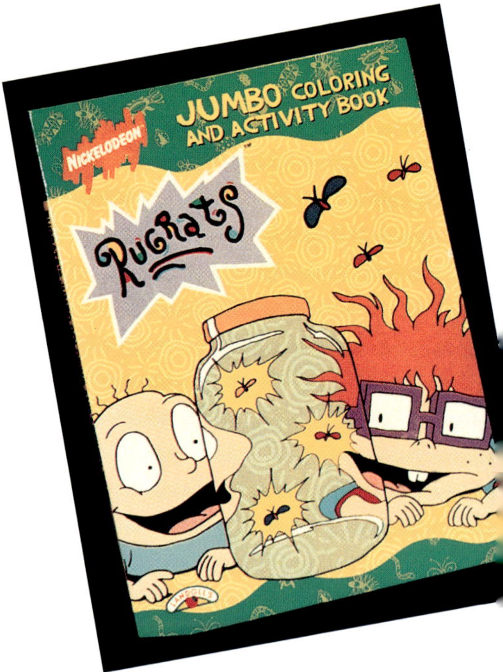

Jumbo Coloring and Activity book. Ladoll's. $3-4

Activity book. Landoll's. $3-4

Painting with water book. Front and back view. $3-4

Super Coloring and Activity book, front and back view. Landoll's. $3-4

Super Coloring and Activity book. Landoll's. $3-4

Coloring and Activity book. Landoll's. $3-4

Super Coloring and Activity book. Landoll's. $3-4

Activity Tablet. Landoll's. $6-8

My Sticker Album. $4-6

The Rugrats Joke Book by David Lewman. $4-6

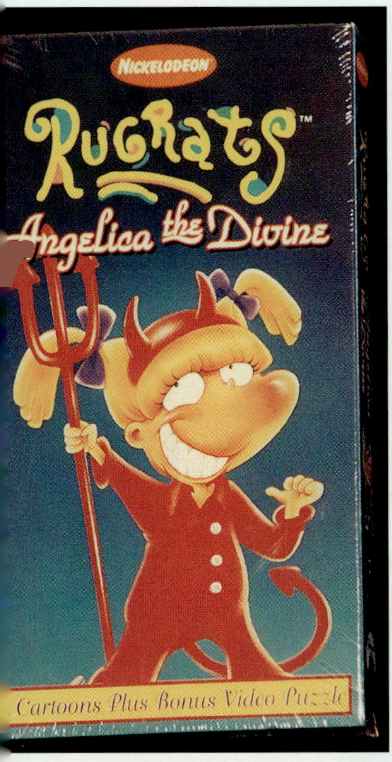

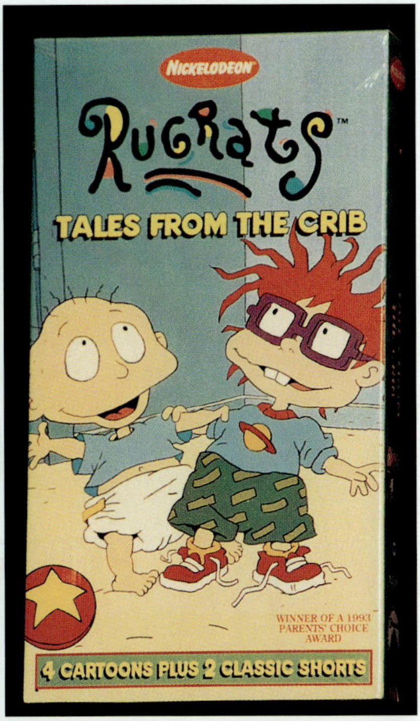

Top left: Rugrats: Angelica The Divine. Paramount Home Video. Includes *Angelica The Magnificent*, *Seven Voyages of Cynthia*, *Runaway Angelica* and *Angelica's Worst Nightmare*. $10-15

Top right: Rugrats: Tales From The Crib. Paramount Home Video. Includes *Toy Palace*, *Real Or Robots?*, *Beach Blanket Babies*, and *The Trial*. $10-15

Bottom left: Rugrats: Chuckie the Brave. Paramount Home Video. Includes *The Slide*, *My Friend Barney*, *Chuckie Vs. The Potty*, and *Chuckie's Wonderful Life*. $10-15

Bottom right: Rugrats: A Baby' s Gotta Do What A Baby's Gotta Do. Paramount Home Video. Includes *Monsters in the Garage*, *Touchdown Tommy*, *Let There be Light*, and *The Inside Story*. $10-15

Partytime and Holidays

Designware paper napkins. American Greetings. $3-4

Eight party invitations. "Come on over and join the party!" Designware. American Greetings. $2-3

Designware paper napkins. American Greetings. $3-4

Eight party thank-you cards. Designware. American Greetings. $2-3

Designware paper napkins. American Greetings. $3-4

Plastic table cover with satin finish. 54" x 96". Designware. American Greetings. $5-7

Eight party gift boxes. Designware. American Greetings. $2-3

Eight 9-oz. paper cups. Designware. American Greetings. $2-3

Party favor viewer key chains. Tara Toy Corp. China. $6-8

Designware 6" and 8" set of eight paper plates. American Greetings. $3-4 each.

Chalk party favors. Tara Toy Corp. China. $6-8

Party favor playing cards. Tara Toy Corp. China. $6-8

Eight blowout party favors. Designware. American Greetings. $2-3

Honeycomb centerpiece. Designware. American Greetings. 8 9/16". $4-6

Designware confetti. American Greetings. $3-4

Designware crepe paper streamer. 10 yards. $2-3

Two mylar balloons on sticks. 9". $3-5 each.

Rugrats package of 30 Valentines. $2-3

Sheet of static cling 12" x 17" window decorations. $3-4

Sheet of static cling window decorations. $2-3

Sheet of static cling window decorations. $2-3

Sheet of static cling window decorations. 12" x 17". $3-4

Sheet of static cling window decorations. $2-3

Sheet of static cling window decorations. $2-3

Plastic suction cup hang-ups. Tommy, Tommy and Spike, Chuckie. $2-3 each.

Package of 20 gift tags. American Greetings. Forget Me Not. $2-3

Rugrat gift paper. Wrapping paper. American Greetings. Forget Me Not. $3-4

Glitter wrap wrapping paper. $10-12 each.

Rugrat wrapping paper. American Greetings. Forget Me Not. $3-4

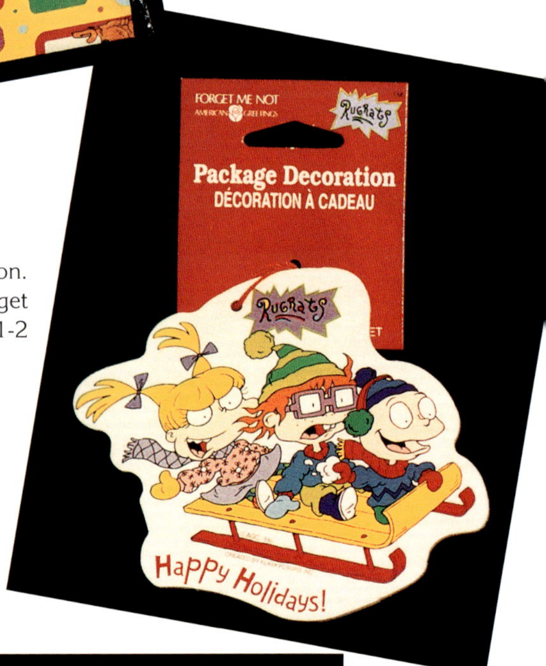

Package decoration. American Greetings. Forget Me Not. $1-2

Tissue paper gift wrap, Reptar design. American Greetings. Forget Me Not. $3-4

Plastic Angelica Christmas ornament. American Greetings. 2.5". $10-15

Plastic Chuckie Christmas ornament. American Greetings. 2.5". $10-15

Plastic Tommy Christmas ornament. American Greetings. 2.5". $10-15

American Greetings paper gift bag. 6" x 8". $3-4

American Greetings paper gift bag. 10" x 13". $6-7

American Greetings paper gift bag. 7" x 10". $4-5

American Greetings paper gift bag.
17" x 24". $7-9

American greetings
paper gift bag. 10" x 12".
$3-5

Schooltime

Paper folder. Tommy laying on top of ball on cover. Stuart Hall Co. $2-3

Paper folder. Tommy and Spike on cover. Stuart Hall Co. $2-3

Paper folder. Chuckie on cover. Stuart Hall Co. $2-3

Paper folder. Rugrat gang on cover. Stuart Hall Co. $2-3

Spiral Notebook. Tommy and Spike on cover. Stuart Hall Co. $5-6

Spiral Notebook. Tommy lying on top of ball on cover. Stuart Hall. $5-6

Spiral Notebook. Chuckie on cover. Stuart Hall Co. $5-6

Spiral Notebook. Rugrat gang on cover. Stuart Hall Co. $5-6

Cardboard binder with Rugrat gang on cover. Stuart Hall Co. $7-10

Cardboard binder with Chuckie, Angelica, and Tommy on cover. Stuart Hall Co. $7-10

Cardboard binder with Chuckie, Spike, Tommy on cover. Stuart Hall Co. $7-10

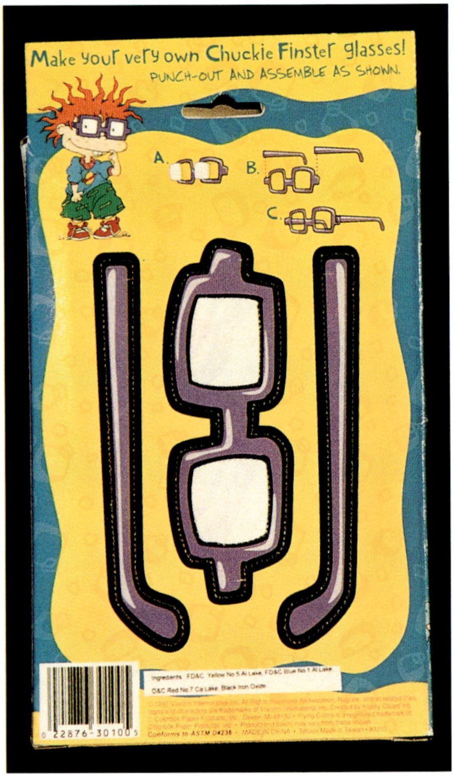

Tommy's Tattoo Parlor. Over 100 tatoos. Flying Colors. Front and back view of box. $6-8

3-D Crayon By Number Activity Kit. Flying Colors. Front and back view of box. $6-8

Picture Stitchers, Sewing Card Activity Set. Front and back view of box. $6-8

Sticker Mix-Ups Activity Set. Front and back view of box. $6-8

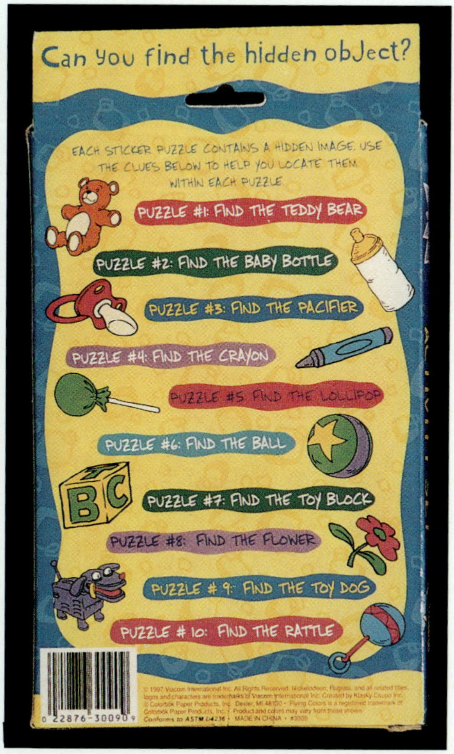

Chuckie magnets. Win Craft Co. Also available featuring other Rugrats characters. $6-8

Designware set of four magnets. American Greetings. $4-5

Package of 5 Rugrats pencils. Sanford Co. $2-3

Package of three colorful rubber erasers. Angelica, Tommy, Chuckie. Sanford Co. $3-4

Box of 5 washable markers. Sanford Co. Made in Italy. $5-7

Pencil Case Activities. Contains three pencils, Tommy eraser, clips, stickers. Flying Colors Co. $4-5

Talking Tommy Drawing Desk. Press his head and he talks. Flying Colors Co. $25-35

Tommy's Art Adventure. Art studio and activity set. Flying Colors Co. $10-15

Set of five Action Stampers and ink pad. Collector's set. Flying Colors Co. $15-20

Set of five Action Stampers and ink pad. Collector's set. Flying Colors Co. $15-20

Single Action Stampers. (Sold seperately) Baby Dil, Reptar, Phil and Lil. $5-6 each.

Package of two Action Stampers. Angelica and Lil. Viacom. $7-10 set

Package of fifteen paper fun bags. In The Bag, Purchase, N.Y. $5-7

Plastic pencil pouch. Handy pocket for pencils and stuff. Fits three-ring binder. Heavy duty zipper. $4-6 each.

Plastic lunch box with thermos. Viacom. $10-15

Diary with lock and key. 145 pages. Stuart Hall Co. $7-10

Sixteen-month calendar. Traditions. Calendar came with mini calendar also. $10-15

Sixteen-month mini calendar, front and back. Traditions. $5-7

Holiday tags. American Greetings. Forget Me Not. $2-3

Two sheets of stickers. Designware. American Greetings. $2-3

Halloween stickers. American Greetings. $2-3 each.

Two sheets of stickers. Designware. American Greetings. $1-2

Two sheets of stickers. American Greetings. $1-2

Nylon umbrella. $8-12

Premiums and Advertising

Free magazine from Burger King. Inside, front, and back. Shows the watches and free toys from Kid's Meals. $3-5

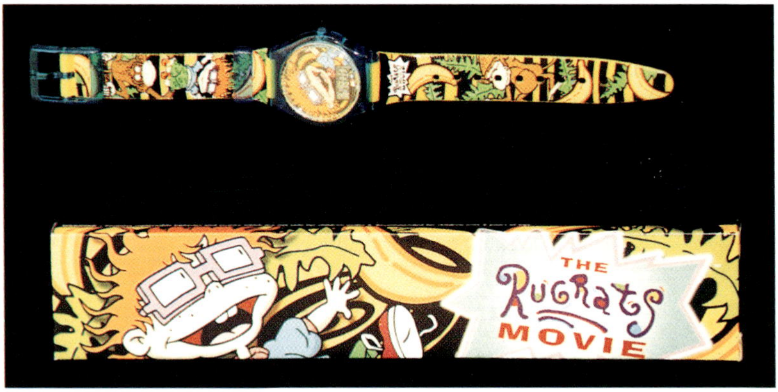

Plastic Chuck Bananarama watch from Burger King. Scratch and sniff, band smells like banana. $15-20. (Sold for $1.99 with purchase from Burger King)

Plastic Reptar watch from Burger king. Tilt it and it moves. Animated action. $15-20. (Sold for $1.99 with purchase from Burger King)

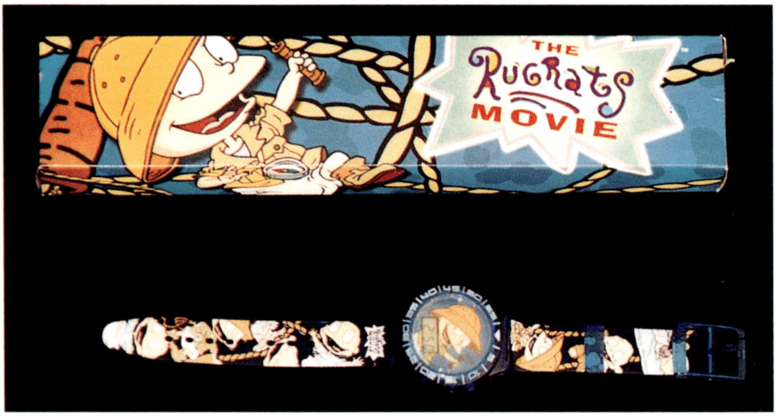

Plastic Touch and Talk Tommy watch from Burger King. Press button and Tommy says "A baby's gotta do what a baby's gotta do." $15-20. (Sold for $1.99 with purchase from Burger King)

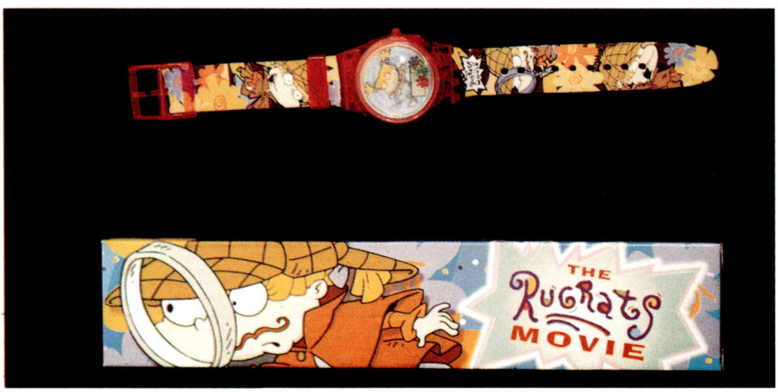

Plastic Angelica's Flower Power watch from Burger King. Shake watch and the flowers float. $15-20. (Sold for $1.99 with purchase from Burger King)

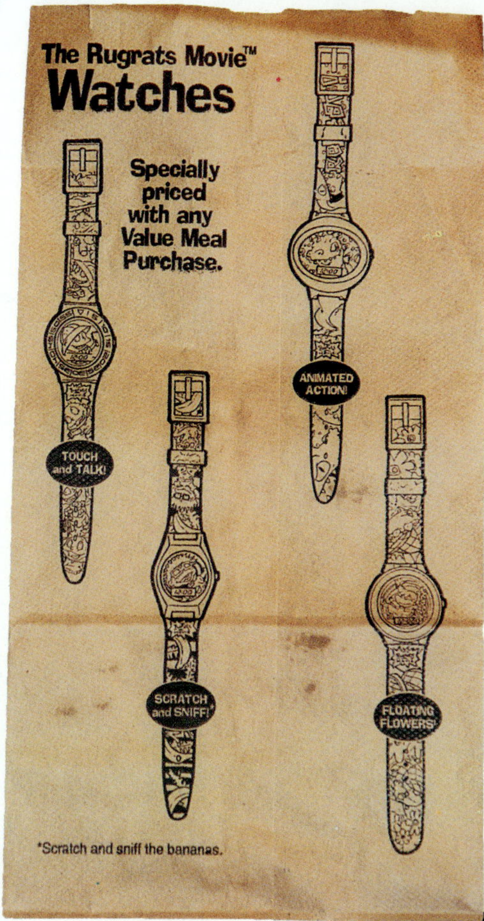

Back of bag shows watches from Burger King.

Plastic #1 Aqua Reptar toy from Burger King Kids Meal. Rolls over land, floats on water. $2-3

Plastic #2 scooting Susie toy from Burger King Kids Meal. Susie takes her scooter for a ride. $2-3. The other toys in the series are #3 Spike on his leash. #4 Chuckie's treasure hunt. #5 Shirley Sherlock Holmes Angelica. #6 Monkey mayhem. #7 Phil and Lil: My Reptar. #8 Baby Dil awakens. #9 Reptar wagon. #10 Dactar glider. #11 Clip on Tommy with Baby Dil. #12 Okey Dokey Tommy. $2-3 each.

Insert paper from Burger King toy package.

Cardboard crown from Burger King. Given free. $3-4

12-oz. paper cup from
Burger King. $1-2

12-oz. paper cup from
Burger King. $1-2.

Paper french fry wrapper from Burger King. $1-2

Paper bag from Burger King. $2-3

Poster advertising Rugrat Movie. Inside and front. $5-7

Poster advertising giveaway from J.C. Penney's. (Great graphics) 28" x 22". $15-20

Cardboard advertising tag from Wal-mart. $3-4

Paper Campbell soup advertiser for soup with Rugrats on label.

Campbell soup with Rugrats on label. $2-3

Campbell chicken with rice soup with Rugrats on label. $2-3

Advertising box from Mott's watermelon apple sauce. (great graphics) $5-10

M & M minis in plastic tube advertising the Rugrats on label. $2-3

Watermelon applesauce with Rugrats on label. $2-3 pack

Post Raisin Bran cereal with advertising for free tickets to the movie. Rugrats on front and back. $4-6

Cheese Lunchables from Oscar Mayer. Rugrats advertising on front and back. $3-4

Post Waffle Crisp cereal with advertising for free movie tickets. $3-4

Printed Comic Book Bubble Gum. Front and back side. (Each piece of gum has a cartoon printed on it) $2-3 each.

Different back sides of the two main bubble gum packages. $2-3 each.

Bubble gum Box. $5-8

Other Rugrat Collectibles Not Shown

Posters from Daydreams, Inc: (An “At A Glance” subsidiary. 1997-1998. Four in this series:

#1 The Rugrats looking at the audience, with Tommy ready to squirt his milk.
#2 Angelica hugging Tommy & Chuckie.
#3 The Rugrats with Reptar.
#4 Tommy, Chuckie and Angelica with Dil.

View Master reels:

#1 The Slide, #2 Circus Angelicus, #3 Baseball or (Stadium Seats).

Food items:

Fruit Snacks from Farley. Macaroni and Cheese from Kraft. Ice Cream sandwich (peanut butter and jelly flavored) from Good Humor. Fruit Rolls (with a Rugrats stamper to make your own impressed fruit rolls, from Farley.

Trade cards by Tempo: 17 Character cards featuring the Rugrats and the adults.

Episode cards: “Touchdown Tommy” and “The Trial”—27 cards each.

Hanging Mobile cards: Nine different cards—make your own Rugrats mobile.

Stand-up cards: Seven different cards featuring the Rugrats and other stand-ups.

Tommy Pickles ceramic cookie jar. Tommy’s hat is the lid. Viacom. $50-75

Talking Tommy cereal bowl. Press on his head and he says “A baby’s gotta eat what a baby’s gotta eat!” Bowl, spoon and plastic doll included. $15-20

Rugrats Backyard Play Set by Colorforms. $5-7

Rugrats Adventure Game by Broderbund. Win/Mac. $30-35

Rugrats Movie Activity Challange by Broderbund. Win/Mac. $30-35

Rugrats Print Shop by Broderbund. Design stickers and stationary with many other projects. $20-25

The Rugrats Movie Game by THQ. Game Boy. $30-35

Rugrats: Search for Reptar by THQ. Sony Play Station. $45-55

Videos

Rugrats: Tommy Troubles by Paramount Home video. Includes s"Naked Tommy," "Incident in Aisle 7," "Baseball Tommy," "Rebel Without a Teddy Bear". $15-20

Rugrats' Bedtime Bash by Paramount Home Video. Includes "Party Animals," "Under Chuckie's Bed," "Tooth and Dare," "In the Dreamtime," "The Last Babysitter". $15-20

Rugrats: Dr. Tommy Pickles by Paramount Home Video. Includes "Hiccups," "Autumn leaves," "Potty Training Spike," "Chicken Props," "Grandpa's Bad Bug". $15-20

A Rugrats Chanukah by Paramount Home Video. Double length movie. 33 minutes. $15-20

Rugrats: A Rugrats Vacation by Paramount Home Video.Includes "Viva Slots Vegas," "Graham Canyon," "Ice Cream Mountain." $15-20

Rugrats: Angelica Knows Best by Paramount Home Video. Includes "Psycho Angelica," "Angelica Knows Best," Angelica's Last Stand," "Ransom of Cynthia," "Word of the Day." $15-20

Rugrats: Return of Reptar by Paramount Home Video. Includes "At The Movies," "Reptar on Ice," "Reptar's Revenge," "Candy Bar Creep Show," "Reptar 2010." $15-20

Rugrats: Mommy Mania by Paramount Home Video. Includes "Mother's Day," "Family Feud," "Game Show Didi," "Mommy's Little Assets." $15-20

Rugrats: Phil & Lil Double Trouble by Paramount Home Video. Includes "Baby Commercial," "Twins Pique," "The Unfair Pair," "Together at Last."

Rugrats: Diapered Duo by Paramount Home Video. Includes "Down the Drain," "The Odd Couple," "Mirrorland," "Give and Take," "Farewell My Friend." $15-20

Rugrats: Grandpa's Favorite Stories by Paramount Home Video. Includes "Grandpa's Date," "Legend of Satchmo," "Grandpa's Teeth," "Visitors from Outer Space," "Grand Moves Out." $15-20

Books

A Baby's Got to Grow book by Sarah Wilson. $7-10

Eat it First, Ask Questions Later book by David Lewman. $3-4

The House That Chuckie Built book by Sarah Wilson. $5-7

The Making of the Movie: Behind the Scenes at Klasky Csupo by Jan Breslauer. $20-25

The Rugrats' Book of Chanukah by Sarah Wilson. $7-8

The Rugrats' Potty Book: A Baby's Got to Go book by Kathi Wagner. $4-5

Space Invaders! by Sarah Albee. $4-5

Tommy Catches a Cold by Sarah Wilson. $3-4

Tommy's New Playmate by David Luke. $3-4

The Turkey Who Came to Dinner by Kitty Richards. $5-7

The Ultimate Rugrat Fan Book by Jefferson Graham. $8-10

Merry Christmas, Rugrats: A lift the flap book with 54 flaps by Kitty Richards. $8-10